DEMI
PRENTISS

Making
Money
Holy

CHURCH
PUBLISHING
INCORPORATED

A little
book of
guidance

Church Publishing
19 East 34th Street
New York, NY 10016
www.churchpublishing.org

Cover design by Jennifer Kopec, 2 Pug Design
Typeset by Denise Hoff

A record of this book is available from the Library of Congress.

ISBN-13: 9781640652224 (pbk.)
ISBN-13: 9781640652231 (ebook)

Printed in Canada

For my husband Paul
For forty-seven years, his sense of humor
and love of adventure
have been our most transformative assets.

Contents

Introduction

Let me assure you, dear reader, that despite the title, *Making Money Holy* will not offer a rite for sprinkling currency with holy water in order to render it holy. Like a hammer or a computer or a paintbrush, money is a tool, and holy is as holy does. That is, the way we use our money is what makes it holy or unholy, life-giving and liberating or death-dealing and oppressing.

That's not to advocate a sort of "works righteousness for things." Putting it to good use does not make it "saved" for eternity or assure its place in heaven. Money is fungible—a canvas that displays our projections. Money as a vehicle for holiness is more a matter of "by their fruit you shall know them" (Matthew 7:16). What our money accomplishes usually indicates whether it's been put to holy or unholy use.

In large measure, our relationship with money shapes how we put it to use. As God's children, we are called to be fully human, bearers of the Christ-light within us. As Micah 6:8 reminds us, the Lord asks that we "do justice, love kindness, and walk humbly with our God." We're called to use our money to those ends.

To help us discern how we might walk that path, this book takes a hard look at money: how it makes us crazy, how we fear it and idolize it, and how we're inclined to exile it from our relationship with God. When we take the risk to engage God, our faith, and the larger community in our money story, we come to recognize where our wealth lies and how we can use our assets in ways that enrich our lives.

I invite you into this conversation about money. I encourage you to discover how the discussion becomes richer and more transformative as you widen it to include a diversity of voices. I pray that you will grow as an agent in your own financial life, as you claim the true value of your assets and of your identity, grounded in God the giver of all.

Demi Prentiss

1 ▪ *Why Are We So Crazy About Money?*

"I don't like money very much, but it calms my nerves."

—Joe Lewis, prizefighter

We *are* crazy about money. We like it, a whole lot. And we do crazy things because of and for and about money. What's that about?

The Water We Swim In

In many respects, the power that money has in our lives—the crazy-making power—springs from the culture that surrounds us. That's true whether we are products of Western European culture, or Asian culture, or African, or Caribbean. As long as we understand money as a way of quantifying our assets, money will be laden with cultural, emotional, psychological, even spiritual freight.

Money as a way of evaluating our well-being is a recent development for Americans. Eli Cook, exploring "How Money Became the Measure of Everything"[1] for *The Atlantic*, explains:

> In the mid-nineteenth century . . . American businesspeople and policymakers started to measure progress in dollar amounts, tabulating social welfare based on people's capacity to generate income.
>
> Until the 1850s . . . the most popular and dominant forms of social measurement in nineteenth-century America (as in Europe) were a collection of social indicators known then as "moral statistics," which quantified such phenomena as prostitution, incarceration, literacy, crime,

1

education, insanity, pauperism, life expectancy, and disease. While these moral statistics were laden with paternalism, they nevertheless focused squarely on the physical, social, spiritual, and mental condition of the American people. For better or for worse, they placed human beings at the center of their calculating vision. Their unit of measure was bodies and minds, never dollars and cents.[2]

In the twentieth century, economic indicators increasingly put a monetary value on many aspects of everyday life. In the present day, a price can be put on nearly any aspect of U.S. culture: economic output, productivity, prison recidivism, the impact of cancer, the benefits of school recess, and more.

Cook concludes:

> Since the mid-twentieth century . . . economic indicators have promoted an idea of American society as a capital investment whose main goal, like that of any investment, is ever-increasing monetary growth. . . . [By] making capital accumulation synonymous with progress, money-based metrics have turned human betterment into a secondary concern. By the early twenty-first century, American society's top priority became its bottom line, [and] net worth became synonymous with self-worth.[3]

Money, according to Keith Hart, in his journal article "From a Cultural Point of View," is "culturally plastic"—open to various interpretations depending on the culture—and endowed with multiple interpretations.[4] For people in the United States, with money-based metrics becoming the measure of "what we're worth" far beyond our bank balance, it's an easy jump to deciding that the more money we have, the better we are. And that way lies madness. Jesus reminds us, "What will it profit them to gain the whole world and forfeit their life?" (Mark 8:36)

What's Not to Like?

We love what money can buy for us. Beyond the material things, it buys influence, prestige, a so-called better life, even friends in some cases. So what's not to like?

Well, clearly, it's that "forfeit your life" part that Jesus was talking about. Money can be like a drug, making us feel giddy and powerful, and believing that everything will be okay. It can make us feel as though we are more important than we really are. It can also make us strung out on the notion that we'll never have "enough," whatever that means; that we must spend all our time and energy corralling more, in order to feel safe and secure. And it can make us afraid—of the future, of other people, of dying too young, or of living too long.

In her book *The Emotional Life of Money*, researcher Mary Cross writes,

> Magnetic resonance images show that making money registers in the brain the same way as getting high on cocaine does, again in the amygdala area of the brain. . . . People can become as addicted to money as they can to food or alcohol or drugs. They try to acquire more of it just to acquire it, even when they have plenty, often sacrificing the long-term satisfactions of friendships and contented families in the process.[5]

Many of us are deeply ambivalent about money. While winning the lottery might seem like salvation of a sort, the many cautionary tales about lottery winners "five years after" point to something vaguely dangerous, perhaps even malevolent, about money. Sudden wealth might not be the Godsend some imagine it will be.

A professor of philosophy, Jacob Needleman is the author of *Money and the Meaning of Life.* He said, "Money today has become like sex was to previous generations. It's damn hard, in fact nearly impossible, to think about money honestly. It has an immense influence on everything we do. Yet few people are able to acknowledge the power of money."[6]

Money has the power to set off our emotions, even for those of us who think that we're not emotional. What happens in your body when you receive an unexpected large bill, or a sudden windfall? Or when you order something on the internet, which turns out to be a piece of junk and not at all what it looked like on your computer? Or when you hear that your work colleague makes way less than—or way more than—what you earn? Even imagining those scenarios can get your heart and mind racing.

Those of us who don't find money a bit unnerving may, instead, be caught in an "I deserve it" fantasy: "I'm a good person, I work hard (unlike so many others), and I've done all the right things. It's my money, and I deserve to do what I want with it." From that point of view, "enough" is just on the other side of the next pay raise. In 2018, a study out of Purdue University published in *Nature Human Behaviour* examined the relationship between happiness and income.[7] The study's lead author Andrew T. Jebb said,

> We found that the ideal income point is $95,000 for life satisfaction and $60,000 to $75,000 for emotional

well-being.... This amount is for individuals and would likely be higher for families.... That might be surprising, as what we see on TV and what advertisers tell us we need would indicate that there is no ceiling when it comes to how much money is needed for happiness, but we now see there are some thresholds.

The *Inc.* magazine article continued,

For the first time, the Purdue study also attempted to capture what income level provides the highest level of life evaluation or life satisfaction, which is more of an overall assessment of how one is doing over the long-term.

Turns out this higher level of overall satisfaction is a little more expensive. In Canada and the United States, an income of $105,000 provides the most life satisfaction, while globally the ideal average income is $95,000.

The study found that exceeding these income thresholds actually seems to reduce levels of happiness and satisfaction. This could be because higher income earners are more driven by material gains and social comparisons that can ironically lower those levels.

"The small decline puts one's level of well-being closer to individuals who make slightly lower incomes, perhaps due to the costs that come with the highest incomes," Jebb explained. "These findings speak to a broader issue of money and happiness across cultures. Money is only a part of what really makes us happy, and we're learning more about the limits of money."[8]

A more recent research report published in 2019 by the American Psychological Association[9] points to the idea that having money brings more happiness than spending it. Bank customers in the United Kingdom scored higher on a "life satisfaction" scale when their bank balance was higher. Above and beyond raw earnings, investments, or indebtedness, people perceived their well-being as related to their access to ready sources of cash. The study draws the conclusion that policymakers "should focus not just on boosting incomes but also on increasing people's ready access to money."

Responding to that study in an interview with The Motley Fool, MaxMyInterest CEO Gary Zimmerman offered that liquidity and personal flexibility seemed more important than income or net worth in gauging how money makes people happy.

> Imagine being stuck in a job you don't love, living paycheck to paycheck. You have no flexibility, no hope of quitting to do something different. . . . Now imagine working in that same job, with a year's worth of salary sitting in cash. You might not quit, but you could. It's that feeling of flexibility, of not being trapped, that is so immensely valuable. Holding cash buys you that flexibility.[10]

Zimmerman added that according to psychology research, "people are happier when they spend money on experiences rather than on objects, especially when the experience brings you closer to people you care about and creates unique memories."[11]

Our culture has created an unconscious bias in nearly all of us, toward using money as a measuring stick. Our self-worth and our self-image are all tied up with money in ways that are tough to untangle. Understanding how we feel about money is an important step in being able to overcome the "crazies." Exploring where our feelings come from can lead us to a more grounded, intentional relationship with the money that flows through our lives. And for many of us, how we relate to our money shapes our interactions with the people we live, work, and worship with, and how they think about money, as well.

Who Do You Trust?

As if the questions of how we get money and how we manage money aren't enough, there's also the question of how money affects us as we choose our friends. Typically, our voluntary associations—like the congregation we worship with, or the club we belong to—are with people of similar incomes. Being with people who seem to be in about the same socio-economic bracket as we are tends to raise our comfort level, while those "above" or "below" make us a bit anxious.

Church consultant Dan Hotchkiss, in his book *Ministry and Money*, quotes part of a conversation he overheard at a church:

> "Do you remember that guy who came to church in a Cadillac? He wore a suit. I said to myself, 'He's not going to fit in here.' He parked right out in front in the visitors' parking, and a couple of people made remarks about whether his car would fit. I can tell you, we never saw him again after that day!"
>
> This was by no means a poor congregation. In fact, it was predominantly upper-middle class. Out of curiosity I checked the parking lot, and sure enough, there were no Cadillacs—only Volvos, Audis, Saabs, and

upper-end Toyotas. Like most congregations, this one had sorted itself out not only by income level but also by automotive taste![12]

People who have high-paying jobs are sometimes regarded with envy and suspicion, as much as admiration. People of limited means may be regarded as shiftless, or not very capable, or disadvantaged, or needy at least as often as they are seen as resourceful and determined.

It's amazing, really. In much of the United States, we are ashamed if we have money, and we're ashamed if we don't have money. As Jacob Needleman observed, in many quarters money has replaced sex as the unmentionable topic.

Why Would We Think That?

Where did you learn about money? As you were growing up, your ideas about money were most likely first shaped by your experiences and conversations in your family of origin—not only first-hand but what you observed and overheard. What did you learn in that first "money school"? Some of the most common:

- "Money doesn't grow on trees."
- "Money is the root of all evil." (a misquote of 1 Timothy 6:10)
- "None of your business" or "We don't talk about things like that."
- "Gotta save all we can."
- "Never enough."
- "You can't take it with you."
- "If ya got it, flaunt it."

Perhaps even more than our families, the culture we live in shapes how we think about money. Gordon Gekko and Occupy Wall Street, Broadway musicals and pop tunes, news outlets and Prosperity Gospel preachers, advertisements and Facebook posts—all have a voice in the stream of information that flows around us. And while we don't absorb it all, many of the messages become embedded in our brains:

- "Greed is good."
- "Money can't buy me love."
- "Money makes the world go around."
- "Wealth is a sign of God's favor."
- "I got plenty of nuthin', and nuthin's plenty for me. . . ."
- "There are things money can't buy."
- "He who has the gold makes the rules."
- "Of all wealth created in 2017, 82 percent went to the world's richest 1 percent."[13]
- "Starbucks will spend $250 million of its corporate tax cut to boost the pay and expand the benefits of its American workers."[14]
- "Oh I gotta have it, Ooh I gotta grab it, Hustle real hard, gotta stack that cabbage, I'm addicted to money."[15]
- "Ain't about the money, it's about the power."[16]

For people of faith, the voice of scripture and tradition speak to us when we think about money—and some of the messages seem contradictory. Some seem to mirror what we hear from the secular world, and some condemn our money choices:

- "It is easier for a camel to go through the eye of a needle than for someone who is rich to enter the kingdom of God." (Matthew 19:24)
- "Blessed are the poor." (Luke 6:20)
- "The love of money is a root of all kinds of evil." (1 Timothy 6:10)
- "The widow's mite" (referring to Mark 12:41–44, Luke 21:1–4)
- "The measure you give will be the measure you get back." (Luke 6:38)
- "God needs our money to do God's work."
- "Stewardship is everything we do after we say, 'I believe.'"
- "St. Swithin's will have to close if you don't help support the budget."
- "Our God is a god of abundance."
- "It is better to give than to receive."

How can we integrate those faith messages with the money messages that are shouted by the culture we swim in?

The Shame of It All

Our relationship with money is complicated. It's so complicated that we tell ourselves all kinds of stories to explain why we have decided that we're "bad at it."

- I'm bad at math.
- I'm irresponsible.
- My parents never taught me anything about money.

- My family had too much/too little money, so I never had to deal with it.
- I'm a liberal arts major.
- I'm bad at handling money because I'm so spiritual/creative/scatter-brained/intense about my work/committed to justice/ignorant about the economy.

The topic of money is intimidating, largely because we have no experience talking about it. We don't even *hear* other people talking about it, because such talk is tacky, or rude, or "not what we do." It's easier just to ignore or avoid or hide from such conversations. Some parents find it easier to have "the talk" about sex with their children than to have honest conversations about how the family handles its money.

This cultural practice reinforces money's status as a taboo subject. So being judged "good at" or "bad at" money has moralistic overtones. It's considered a mark of good or bad character. Carl Richards, founder of the Society for Real Financial Planners and a *New York Times* columnist, remarked, "Money is not a math problem. It's a proxy for our moral foundations, our most cherished dreams and our deepest fears."[17]

Money coach Tammy Lally, in her TED Talk, "Money Shame: The Silent Killer," says,

> Our self-destructive and self-defeating financial behaviors are not driven by our rational, logical minds. They are a product of our subconscious belief systems, rooted in our childhoods and so deeply ingrained in us, they shape the way we deal with money our entire adult lives. So

> many of you are left believing you're lazy, crazy, or stupid, or just bad with money. This is what I call money shame.[18]

Shame seems to be a common theme related to money. Shame researcher Brené Brown is frequently quoted as saying, "If you put shame in a petri dish, it needs three ingredients to grow exponentially: secrecy, silence, and judgment." In a culture of "don't ask, don't tell" on the subject of money, with a high value placed on financial standing, there's lots of shame in not keeping up with those we consider our peers.

Lally names symptoms of money shame: playing the big shot, always picking up the check; living in a state of chronic not enoughness, despite being financially secure; driving a Mercedes while being able to afford only a Honda; and looking good—at all costs. And there are others, of course. All of them are based in hiding our true situation, meaning living inauthentically. And that's the root and the symptom of madness.

One of the ways we can learn to live in a saner relationship with our finances is by learning to look at money—and talk about money—honestly. That practice can help us deal with the power that money seems to hold in our lives. Since money can touch us so deeply and exert such power over our lives, our well-being may hinge on discovering whether—and how—money might be holy.

2 ▪ *Can We Talk? Honestly?*

"Too many people spend money they haven't earned, to buy things they don't want, to impress people that they don't like."

—*Will Rogers*

I vividly remember the first truly honest conversation my husband and I had about money. We'd been married about fifteen years. Up until that point, we had always worked together—not in the same office, but for the same employer, doing jobs that complemented each other. In the professional theatre, he was a set designer and stage director; I was a stage manager and lighting designer. In community weekly newspapers, he was publisher and I was editor. We had had responsibility for budgets, at work and at home, but we had always been paid by "the company," which was owned by our bosses. Now, for the first time, we were running our own show—a print shop, with him doing the business side and me running the front of shop and supervising our pressman.

Exploring Our Money Stories

At the time, we belonged to a strong, diverse Christian community. One of our friends, a successful businessman, ran a counseling service that focused on couples who ran family businesses together. We were struggling a bit in our business. We didn't have much experience running a small press. And struggling financially was kind of our way of life: not going without meals or getting evicted, but always wrestling with the checkbook, making things do and patching things up rather than buying new, carrying a balance on the credit card that seemed to creep higher.

We were the only full-service print shop in our town of about four thousand people, and we wanted to increase business. Our son, age seven, was growing and enjoying small-town life. Our daughter, his half-sister, was attending a college nearby. We needed our income to grow and to accommodate family expenses. Though we never fought, verbally or physically, the tensions around money being so tight were wearing us out.

We arranged to meet with our friend to gain his insight and to improve our business and family lives. Before we had our first meeting, he asked us about our marriage. When we told him, he chuckled. "Among the people I see, they never have any troubles in their marriages; they always just displace them into their business."

Seated in his office, he asked us, "What do you think money is?"

Ever the extravert, I jumped in, "Well, it's a tool. It helps you get things done. You use it to make things better."

My husband was quiet for what seemed like a long time. Finally, he said, "Money is evil." There it was, plain as day! I don't remember what he said next.

While I was trying to corral money and hang onto it, my kind, loving, caring life partner was avoiding it, or spending it as a necessary evil because it threatened his soul. No wonder we were struggling to have any.

Our counselor pressed on. "And, in your family growing up, who paid the bills?"

"My dad, of course," I said.

"My mom, of course," my husband answered.

There it was, again. Our two money stories, which we had never told each other, or even thought much about, were colliding. In our marriage, I had nearly always been the one to pay our family bills and do the juggling act, when required, of who got paid this month. I figured it was only fair for me to do that. Both of us worked full time. Generally, my husband worked with the company books during the day, and I knew he hated it. I also hated that chore. I hated feeling unequal to the money management task and uneducated about money. At the same time, I hated not having a handle on where our money was, which happened when my husband paid the family bills. And besides, when we were in a real pinch, I could tap into the money my dad had left me.

I wish I could say that our conversations around money and our business led us to a dramatic shift in the way we related to our money. I can't say that. At least, it was a start in my learning to have a sense of agency about my financial life. That increasing sense of self led to intentional career moves that increased our income, and a realization that we needed to be proactive in planning our financial futures, with the help of a trusted financial planner. If we had not been blessed with good friends and good health all along the way, our story could have been financially disastrous. We were shielded, largely by good fortune, from the consequences of our naiveté.

What If You're Bad with Money?

Unfortunately, my lack of financial training and my sense of money management inadequacy are not all that uncommon. In 2018, *The New York Times* launched "Personal Finance Week," featuring a daily series titled "What to Do When You're Bad at Money." As a part of that series, Kristin Wong wrote,

> We're discouraged from talking about money at every turn, but if you want to fix your financial situation, talking about it is necessary.
>
> Even setting aside that social taboo of discussing money, there are practical hurdles in your way to getting better at money: Learning about money is intimidating, and there's no structural system in place to teach us. Further still, we look at poor money skills as something to be ashamed and embarrassed of, which can keep us from being honest about money and seeking out the right kind of help.[19]

Wong pointed out that a lack of culturally accepted financial metrics makes talking about money especially difficult. She quoted Shannon McLay, a former financial advisor who left Merrill Lynch to launch The Financial Gym, a financial planning firm in Manhattan. "We all know physical health numbers, like BMI, weight, and clothing sizes, so we can assess where we fall on that spectrum," said McLay. "Because of a lack of agreed upon financial metrics, people feel fear or shame around what their finances look like." Wong added,

> All of these forces—the social taboo, the intimidation factor, embarrassment—conspire to keep us from talking about money and improving our circumstances. For example, according to data from Fidelity Investments, 43 percent of Americans don't know how much money their spouse makes, yet fighting about money is a top

predictor of divorce. When you don't even know your household income, you can pretty much guarantee a financial fight will eventually erupt.[20]

Our assumptions about money, embedded in our individual money stories, make talking about money even more difficult. It's not uncommon for us to assume people think about money the same way we do, without realizing that the most powerful influence on that thinking is our childhood experience—far beyond the explicit lessons taught to us. Financial psychologists Brad and Ted Klontz coined the term "money script" to describe the power of those stories in our lives.

> Money scripts . . . are core beliefs about money that drive financial behaviors. Money scripts are typically unconscious, developed in childhood, passed down from generation to generation within families and cultures, contextually bound, and often only partial truths. When money scripts are developed in response to an emotionally charged, dramatic, or traumatic personal, family, or cultural financial flashpoint, such as significant losses during the Great Depression, parental abandonment, or financial bailouts by a family member, money scripts can become resistant to change, even when they are self-destructive.[21]

Wong referred to Klontz's work in naming four common money scripts:

- **Money Vigilance**: when you're super careful with money, and the script we should strive for.

- **Money Avoidance**: when you convince yourself money isn't important and you don't care about it.
- **Money Status:** when you equate self-worth with net worth.
- **Money Worship:** when you think having more money will solve all of your problems.[22]

Klontz added that the avoidance, status, and worship behaviors tended to be associated with lower levels of net worth, lower income, and higher amounts of revolving credit. While "money vigilant" behaviors tended to protect against poor financial health and destructive financial behaviors, they can also lead to anxiety, particularly about having enough money in case of an emergency. "Everyone's habits with money are going to be different. If you want to improve yours, it's crucial to understand your relationship with money and how you approach it so you can pinpoint bad habits. If you don't deal with the emotional side of money management, the practical stuff might not work."[23] Wong's piece on learning how to talk about money offers these main points:

> **Break the silence.** It's hard to learn about something when you're discouraged from talking about it. In that way, silence becomes a tool for oppression. . . .
>
> **Start small.** If you're intimidated by personal finance and unsure of where to start, remember that you don't have to learn everything about money at once. . . .
>
> **Schedule money meetings.** It's important to make sure you and your partner or spouse are on the same financial page. . . . Pick a regular time to hold money meetings

and talk about any financial goals, setbacks, and habits. This will help you avoid fighting about those topics in the future. . . .

Talk to your friends. The more comfortable you are talking about topics like retirement plans, student loans, and budgeting openly among your peers, the more opportunity you have to learn from each other. . . .

Be more honest about money. When your friends invite you out for sushi, it's easy to skirt the issue with an excuse. . . . Try being honest about where you stand with your finances instead. This also creates the possibility for learning. Maybe your friend tells you how she paid off her loan early, for example. Or maybe she just starts suggesting cheaper hangout alternatives.

Set a goal. Having a plan for your money may be the best way to get comfortable with it.

Find like-minded people. When you're trying to get more comfortable with money, it helps to surround yourself with people who are on the same page, who have similar goals and are open to talking about those goals.[24]

Talking About Money Is Essential

"Finding like-minded people" is crucial when you begin to be ready to share your thoughts about money. For some of us, a less risky first step can be to listen in on money conversations. Podcasts are typically free and offer great learning opportunities. There is a wide variety, ranging from the big economic picture to specific needs. You can find podcasts focusing on niche audiences that range from beginners in finance, to those in debt, to women, to those seeking to finance higher education, or buy a house, or grow their investments, or develop passive income.

Once you've listened a bit, you'll be better equipped to begin to have conversations with whoever might be a partner in your financial life. Your life partner, if you have one, will be at the top of that list. Talking about money is, without a doubt, difficult for many people. But not talking about money is an almost certain road to disagreement, disappointment, anger, and breakup.

In financial conversations, "fear, shame, and anger are the three internal obstacles," according to Suze Orman, personal finance expert and author of *The Do's and Don'ts of Money*.[25] *New York Times* writer Maria Teresa Hart reports, "Researchers have shown there's a direct relationship between the number of times a couple has argued about their budget per month and their divorce rate."[26] Some couples schedule financial conversations in much the same way that they schedule regular "date nights."

What does "talking about money" mean? As Klontz's "money scripts" remind us, sharing early experiences of money can lay important groundwork. And beyond "Did you pay the light bill?" additional important topics include:

- How do our daily expenses so far this month line up with the monthly total we intend to spend?
- What are our financial priorities for the coming year?
- What are our financial values and our long-term goals?[27]

The topics may not sound threatening or emotional. But when money is the topic, every one of us is a bundle of conscious and unconscious, settled and unresolved feelings:

> Money . . . is a blank slate just waiting for us to write on it, as the Jungian analysts point out. It becomes the stand-in for our feelings of security, power, and status, augmenting them. And we tend to use our money to treat those feelings. That might mean "Spend it like you got it" for one person, who maxes out the credit cards; for another, it manifests in socking away every penny, no questions asked. Money also generates strong feelings of anxiety and despair, both about having it and about not having it. People kill for money, marry for money, rob and steal for money. . . . It can motivate the highest and the lowest levels of human behavior.[28]

Targeting couples, David Weliver offers his thoughts about "having the talk" for the website Money Under 30. He emphasizes keeping the tone light and casual, starting slow, and being understanding. He lists six significant guidelines:

1. Agree to disagree. Men and women value **money** differently.

2. Don't make it a big deal.

3. Focus on each other's strengths.

4. Don't just **talk** numbers, **talk** values.

5. Do. Not. Lie.

6. **Talk** about earning **money**, not just spending it.[29]

Prioritizing the relationship means being willing to support your partner's efforts and offering a bit of grace, as well as remembering that each individual needs to discover their own "hacks" for creating good money habits.

In addition to your life partner, a trusted financial planner—recommended to you by people whose money expertise you trust—is also a person to talk to. Many financial transactions, such as choosing how to structure a retirement account, can involve unseen implications that are often not apparent on the surface and that may have long-term consequences. A financial advisor is trained to have that broader overview and apply it to the client's unique situation. That said, not everyone needs a paid financial advisor. In an article for *U.S. News*, Geoff Williams and Coryanne Hicks quote financial advisor Nicole Rutledge Regilio: "Once someone is to the point that they have stable and steady income and have the ability to save at least 20 percent of their annual income, it might be time to consider a financial advisor."[30]

Until you've reached that point, developing the habit of saving is essential. And even when it's the right time to consider a financial advisor, not everyone may choose to hire one. The decision involves several important steps:

1. Decide if you need a human **financial advisor**. Financial advisory firms and online services can provide assistance. Likewise, robo advisors can be a great option.

2. Determine the type of **advisor** you want. The financial industry has two sets of compliances that advisors follow called the suitability standard or the fiduciary standard. A good credential to look for is the CFP, or certified financial planner.

3. Get referrals from friends or Google. Ask people with a similar financial situation or goals to yours who they use. Take down a few names, then head back to good ol' Google to check the advisor out.

4. Check the **financial advisor's** credentials. Verify your advisor's credentials on brokercheck.com or adviserinfo.sec.gov. The CFP Board also maintains a list of disciplined CFPs by state on their website.

5. Interview multiple advisors. When you do talk to advisors, ask them to "describe their client experience," says Andrew Crowell, vice chairman of D.A. Davidson & Co. Wealth Management in Los Angeles. "How frequently and how will they communicate with you? How do they measure 'success' in a client relationship? Do you need to fit into their model, or are they able to customize an approach to your individual preferences and needs?"

   Ask about the other resources available to you as a client. "No one can be an expert in all aspects of financial matters," Crowell says. "Knowing your advisor has access to specialized expertise" can reassure you that you won't "'outgrow' your advisor's capabilities."

   Be upfront with what you bring to the table, too. ... To that end, [Regilio says,] "share an overview of your financial situation as well as what you hope to achieve with the advisor."[31]

Beyond talking, there are many avenues for becoming more savvy about money. Web-based resources, especially those aimed at beginners in money management, offer low-cost and easy-access lessons via blogs, podcasts, e-books, and news stories. Many provide templates and worksheets that can help you begin to take charge of the money that passes through your hands.

The Simplified Version

When Harold Pollack, a University of Chicago professor of social administration, confronted a sudden increase in his financial obligations, he realized he needed a crash course in personal financial management. He immersed himself in literature on investing, as well as blogging for "The Reality-Based Community." His blog led him to interview finance experts.

> In 2013, Pollack interviewed personal finance writer Helaine Olen about her book, *Pound Foolish*. During their online video chat, Pollack shared his views on personal finance advice and what Pollack calls the "financial industry's most basic dilemma."
>
> "[The best personal finance advice] can fit on a 3-by-5 index card, and is available for free in the library," Pollack said during the interview. "So, if you're paying someone for advice, almost by definition, you're probably getting the wrong advice because the correct advice is so straightforward."
>
> After Pollack posted the video, he started receiving emails asking where to find this index card and what was the advice.
>
> The problem: the index card didn't exist.

So, Pollack grabbed an index card from his daughter, wrote several personal finance principles, snapped a photo with his phone and posted it online. The actual index card was 4-by-6 inches (rather than 3-by-5).

The result: the photo went viral.[32]

The viral post led to Pollack and Olen collaborating to create their book *The Index Card*, explaining the principles behind Pollack's nine simple index card rules:

1. Strive to save 10 to 20 percent of your income.
2. Pay your credit card balance in full every month.
3. Max out your 401(k) and other tax-advantaged savings accounts.
4. Never buy or sell individual stocks.
5. Buy inexpensive well-diversified mutual funds and exchange-traded funds.
6. Make your financial advisor commit to the fiduciary standard.
7. Buy a home when you are financially ready.
8. Insurance: Make sure you're protected.
9. Do what you can to support the social safety net.
10. Remember the index card.[33]

The *Freakonomics* podcast featuring Pollack continues:

A lot of recent social-science research suggests that reminders like this, nudges like this, are pretty effective. Also: one reason people often fail to make good decisions—financial or otherwise—is because those decisions are too complicated or intimidating. So: simplicity is a thing to strive for. And to value. Will a simplified choice always lead to optimal outcomes? Of course not. But will it generally produce a better outcome than either avoiding the problem or doing something really stupid? Yes, it will.[34]

Choosing to Grow Toward Wholeness

While the principles are straightforward, becoming a knowledgeable financial consumer takes work, and there's almost always something new to learn. The ability to engage different people in conversations about money can be one of your best tools.

Cultivating multiple strategies for talking about and learning more about money works to combat the cultural attitudes that connect money and shame. As Keith Hart mentions in his cultural study of money, "Money . . . is not a thing, but a process through which people configure their human associations."[35]

Christian tradition frames the issue in a similar way:

> Money isn't the problem, our relationship with it is. "Love of money," not money, "is the root of all kinds of evil," 1 Timothy 6:10 records. The financial part of our life and all that it represents is important and is meant to serve us, but we too often end up serving it. And it isn't just God that gets displaced; it's relationships, health, curiosity, integrity . . . the list goes on.[36]

The toxicity of "money shame" impacts most areas of our lives, if we allow it. Unlike guilt, which focuses on things we've done or failed to do, shame addresses our very identity. While guilt can motivate change, shame can be destructive and paralyzing. Many feel shame when our financial situation is the way we measure ourselves against our peers.

In her book *Daring Greatly*, Brené Brown writes, "I define vulnerability as uncertainty, risk, and emotional exposure," and, "If we can share our story with someone who responds with empathy and understanding, shame can't survive."[37] Brown's research indicates that money conversations are important tools to foster our growth in taking charge of our financial lives.

Maggie Germano draws on Brown's insights to offer these recommendations:

- Talk to your loved ones about money. The more we open up about something, the less isolated and ashamed we will feel.

- Forgive yourself for your past decisions.

- Make a list of everything you've done well. It doesn't just have to relate to money, it can be anything. However, an additional step can be to show how you can apply that action to a financial activity.

- Recognize that your mistakes can teach you how to do better.

- Choose small things you can start doing now. Here are some ideas:

  » Make a list of all of your monthly expenses, so that you know exactly how much needs to go out every month.

  » Sign up for a budget tracking platform like Mint, YNAB, or ClarityMoney.

> » Take a money minute at least once a week,
>   where you sit down to review your spending
>   and compare it to your monthly budget.

- Work with a professional—a therapist, a coach, or
  a financial planner.[38]

Notably, the first and last suggestions recommend actual, live conversations with other people. All the other items entail an internal conversation, leading to acknowledging mistakes, self-forgiveness, affirmation, and deliberately choosing new behaviors.

None of these is easy. They are steps along the way to creating a healthy relationship with our money. Growing into wholeness with respect to money involves learning to allow ourselves to be vulnerable—to take risks, and fail, and find the courage to risk again, learning along the way. As painful as that process can be, it opens us to building relationships with our community and with God. In that sense, in addition to being a tool to do work, money can serve as a pathway for growing into the full stature of Christ.

Brené Brown offers encouragement for those with the courage to admit their vulnerability and risk undertaking that journey to wholeness:

> I think the people who wade into discomfort and vulnerability and tell the truth about their stories are the real badasses in this world. This is especially true of people who rumble with failure. These are people who choose courage over comfort, accountability over blame, and are able to embed key learnings from failures into their lives. . . . The difference between *I am a screwup* and *I screwed up* may look small, but in fact it's huge. Many of

us will spend our entire lives trying to slog through the shame swampland to get to a place where we can give ourselves permission to both be imperfect and to believe we are enough.

Failure can become our most powerful path to learning if we're willing to choose courage over comfort.[39]

Learning to be more courageous and more willing to travel the bumpy path can be key to becoming honest with ourselves and with others about the role money plays in our lives. Becoming more whole is one of the rewards of that journey, and the path to wholeness often involves exploring the role of our "higher power"—and what we understand that higher power to be. When money can be the "outward and visible sign" that sets us on that journey toward wholeness, money can be holy.

3 ▪ *What's God Got to Do with It?*

"Money is a great servant but a bad master."
—Francis Bacon

Back in chapter one, we looked at a list of quotes that many in contemporary culture, whether Christian or not, seem to know and quote from scripture:

- "It is easier for a camel to go through the eye of a needle than for someone who is rich to enter the kingdom of God." (Matthew 19:24)
- "Blessed are the poor." (Luke 6:20)
- "The love of money is a root of all kinds of evil." (1 Timothy 6:10)
- "The widow's mite." (referring to Mark 12:41–44, Luke 21:1–4)
- "The measure you give will be the measure you get back." (Luke 6:38)

It almost seems that scripture is saying wealth is not something God-fearing people are supposed to have.

The Burden of Inexhaustible Wealth

Most people seem to interpret much of what they read in the Bible as "Money bad; God good," which sets up the notion that God doesn't like money. It's all too easy to draw the conclusion, "Rich bad; poor good." But our life experience tells us that many people who have the ability to earn lots of money also have the gift of using it well, for the common good. People like Microsoft founder

Bill Gates and renowned investor Warren Buffett spring to mind. Both are billionaires. The Bill and Melinda Gates Foundation focuses on aiding children around the world. Largely through the foundation, Gates has earned the reputation of being one of the most generous people in the world as well as one of the richest, having donated more than $45 billion as of 2019.[40] Buffett and Gates have collaborated to challenge their peers to join them in The Giving Pledge,[41] a commitment to give away more than half their wealth. More than two hundred other wealthy couples and individuals have chosen to join Buffett and Gates, leveraging their philanthropy to address some of the world's biggest challenges.

The Giving Pledge is not a religion-based undertaking; it "came to life following a series of conversations with philanthropists around the world about how they could collectively set a new standard of generosity among the ultra-wealthy."[42] As Bill Gates explains, "This is about building on a wonderful tradition of philanthropy that will ultimately help the world become a much better place."[43] As the pledge's website explains:

> The Giving Pledge is a simple concept: an open invitation for billionaires, or those who would be if not for their giving, to publicly dedicate the majority of their wealth to philanthropy. And it is inspired by the example set by millions of people at all income levels who give generously—and often at great personal sacrifice—to make the world better. Envisioned as a multi-generational effort, the Giving Pledge aims over time to help shift the social norms of philanthropy toward giving more, giving sooner, and giving smarter.[44]

Those two hundred billionaires are about 10 percent of the number of billionaires worldwide.[45] As the pledge approaches its tenth anniversary, analysis of both the pledge and its outcomes has been disappointing to many. The difficulties of giving money away well and targeting philanthropy to impact the world's most pressing problems are not addressed in the pledge itself, nor in its infrastructure. The Gates Foundation has organized gatherings to help philanthropists do more good with their money, but impacts are hard to measure. The absence of accountability and transparency has been criticized. Analysts assess the results of the pledge, ten years after its founding, as modest—not nearly fulfilling its initial promise. Marc Gunther, in *The Chronicle of Philanthropy*,[46] writes,

> The vast majority of the ultrarich, in the United States and abroad, have taken a pass [on signing the pledge]. Nor has the pledge inspired greater generosity among all Americans. While charitable giving in the United States has grown along with the economy, total giving by individuals, foundations, and business adds up to about 2 percent of gross domestic product. It's been stuck at that level for decades.
>
> A 2018 report from the Bridgespan Group focusing on about 2,000 of the very wealthiest American families—those with assets of $500 million or more—found that they donated about 1.2 percent of their assets to charity in 2017. That's a lot of money: $45 billion, give or take. It's not enough, however, to keep pace with the growth in their assets.

The result is that these very wealthy families, as a group, are piling up wealth faster than they are giving it away, even in the face of pressing problems that philanthropy could tackle—climate change, global poverty, a tide of refugees, neglected tropical diseases, and the suffering caused by dementia and mental illness, to name just a few.[47]

Where Is Your Heart?

It seems that even the desire to "keep up with the Gateses" is not enough to inspire the rich to give away their wealth. Even those who are bottomlessly wealthy are practically unable to give away more than a fraction of their assets. That harks back to the 2019 American Psychological Association study findings mentioned in chapter one, that having money can be more rewarding, emotionally and psychologically, than spending it. Perhaps outgrowing our preoccupation with possessing wealth requires motivation beyond a desire to be known for our philanthropy.

Once we begin interacting intentionally with money, even a modest amount, it doesn't take long to discover that it seems to have a power of its own. Even when we have implemented all the strategies and best practices talked about in chapter two, our own savvy and willpower don't seem to be enough to combat the barrage of money messages that our culture broadcasts. Trying to pull ourselves up by our own bootstraps (which is impossible—consider the physics) gets us nowhere. Since we Christians claim that God has created all that is, there is value in exploring how we might partner with God to develop a more satisfying relationship with our money.

"Where your treasure is, there your heart will be also." These words attributed to Jesus (Matthew 6:21) crop up frequently whenever money is mentioned, especially when a worthy cause is asking for support. Christians are accustomed to hearing these words nearly every year when the annual giving campaign seeks funding for their church's work.

Those words ring true. Once we invest ourselves in something or someone—whether we use money, or time, or imagination, or any other treasured "currency" we have to offer—we find that we tend to pay a lot more attention to how our investment is doing: growing or shrinking, building or languishing, bringing life or remaining stagnant. If you buy penny stocks, if you bet on a football team, if you make a GoFundMe donation, if you back a political candidate, if you support cancer research—the very act of putting money on the table "invests" us in the outcome. Fundraisers of all stripes know that. Your interest may have been caught by something related to a memory or a relationship, but once you have actually made an investment of time or money to advance the cause, your sense of ownership increases.

In his heart/treasure analogy, Jesus seems to be pointing toward something even deeper, saying, essentially, your heart *is* what you treasure. We are what we eat, and our heart—the part of us that makes our pulse race—*is* the very thing we hold most dear.

Jesus wants the thing we most treasure, the thing that lies at the core of our being, to be love: love for God, for neighbor, and for self. He is explicit about it (Mark 12:30–31), quoting Hebrew scripture in what he calls the "great commandment": "You shall *love* the Lord your God with all your heart, and with all your soul, and with all your mind, and with all your strength . . . [and] your neighbor as yourself" (italics mine).

The gospel accounts show Jesus dealing with money more often than any other subject, including love:

- Sixteen out of thirty-eight of Jesus's parables deal with money and possessions.
- Nearly 25 percent of Jesus's words in the New Testament deal with biblical stewardship.
- One out of ten verses in the Gospels deal with money.
- In the Bible, there are more than two thousand scriptures on tithing, money, and possessions, which is twice as many as faith and prayer combined.[48]

Jesus talks a lot about money, because in many ways money—and the ways we choose to use it—reveals who we are. It reveals our values and our attachments. Jesus's reminder "Where your treasure is, there your heart will be also" (Matthew 6:21, Luke 12:34) captures that truth. Or as *The Message* translation says, "The place where your treasure is, is the place you will most want to be, and end up being." The people of first-century Palestine seem not so different from those in twenty-first-century culture.

What Does Scripture Say?

In *Money and Possessions*, Old Testament scholar Walter Brueggemann offers six ideas that provide the framework for the Bible's wisdom on wealth. According to Brueggemann, scripture says that money and possessions:

1. Are gifts from God.
2. Are received as reward for obedience.

3. Belong to God and are held in trust by human persons in community.

4. Are sources of social injustice.

5. Are to be shared in a neighborly way.

6. Are seductions that lead to idolatry.

He observes that each of these ideas "voices a clear contradiction to the conventional wisdom of the ancient world and . . . contradicts the uncriticized wisdom of market ideology."[49] Each of the ideas grows out of the aspirational community commitments that were hallmarks of Jewish culture throughout scripture, and they embody the prioritization of "the common good" over individual desires. "The common good" is a biblical concept that points to the reign of God. As one posting on the *Christianity Today* website defines it:

> *The common good* is the *conditions* necessary for everyone to flourish; it is not a utopian ideal or something to be imposed by one group on another. The *common good* promotes: human dignity, relationships, participation, and stewardship. It insists that everyone is included, no one is left behind. This task is too big for governments alone—we all have a responsibility towards each other.[50]

Brueggemann goes on to list six contradictions that emerge directly from those six fundamental ideas about wealth—that is, money and possessions (M&P):

1. To view M&P as gifts from God contradicts market ideology in which there are no gifts, no free lunches . . .

2. To view M&P as reward for obedience is too readily transposed into the reward system of the market . . .

3. To view M&P as a trust from God contradicts the pretension of market ideology that imagines . . . that "my money is my own; I earned it and can do with it what I want."

4. To view M&P as a source of injustice is to contradict the easy assumptions of the market that autonomous wealth is not connected to the community . . .

5. To view M&P as resources to be shared in a neighborly way contradicts the market assumption that there are no neighbors; there are only rivals, competitors, and threats . . .

6. To view M&P as seductions that lead to idolatry contradicts the market view that M&P are inert and innocent neutral objects.[51]

As Brueggemann makes clear, the Bible's ideas about money were, and still are, counter-cultural. He writes in the introduction,

> My task has been reportage about the texts. I have found, however, that the texts themselves pressed in the direction of advocacy. . . . The large sweep of the text suggests a critical exposé of an economy of extraction whereby

concentrated power serves to extract wealth from vulnerable people in order to transfer it to the more powerful. That extraction is accomplished by the predatory if legal means of tax arrangements, credit and loan stipulations, high interest rates, and cheap labor.[52]

In his review of Brueggemann's book, Stephen Hiemstra remarks, "In today's economy in the United States, where downward mobility has replaced upward mobility for about 80 percent of the population, offering godly guidance on money and possessions is a very practical concern."[53]

What Does God Expect Us to Do?

More than thirty years ago, current events were evoking many of the same concerns expressed in Brueggemann's comments and in scripture. In 1987, Felix G. Rohatyn wrote an op-ed for *The New York Times*:

> I am an investment banker. For the last two years, many of the best and brightest in my business have been pleading guilty to illegal acts and marching off to jail. Successful, wealthy, intelligent men turned out to be greedy, arrogant, and corrupt.
>
> Whereas making things, and the activities related to products, were the main preoccupation of prior generations, making money, and the activities related to money, are the driving forces of our society today.
>
> To be wealthy is not sinful; nor is poverty a virtue. But the pursuit of wealth and power is so pervasive today as to create something that may be entirely new—namely,

a money culture. When such a culture grows cheek-by-jowl with extreme poverty, it is potentially dangerous.[54]

"Becoming Beloved Community" is a 2017 initiative of the Episcopal Church toward racial healing, reconciliation, and justice. Martin Luther King Jr. envisioned "the Beloved Community" as "a realistic, achievable goal that could be attained by a critical mass of people committed to and trained in the philosophy and methods of nonviolence."[55] The vision document for that Episcopal Church initiative says,

> Beloved Community is the practical image of the world we pray for when we say, "Thy kingdom come, thy will be done, on earth as it is in heaven." We dream of communities where all people may experience dignity and abundant life, and see themselves and others as beloved children of God. We pray for communities that labor so that the flourishing of every person (and all creation) is seen as the hope of each. Conceived this way, Beloved Community provides a deeply faithful paradigm for transformation, formation, organizing, advocacy, and witness.[56]

Like all of creation, we are invited to participate in God's "Beloved Community." We are called not only to recognize that, but to participate in the realization of God's reign in every way we can. We grow in becoming agents of God's in-breaking reign when we acknowledge the value that God recognizes in each creature and each person—including ourselves. The Genesis 1:26 affirmation that human beings were created in the image and likeness of God bears witness to the value God places on humanity.

Scripture and Christian tradition, taken as a whole, declare that when we value anything, including money, over God, we are breaking relationship—not only with God, but with our families, our communities, ourselves, and all of creation. Idolatry is the ultimate betrayal of God's relationship with humanity. Because "right relationship" means putting God first, setting ultimate value on any thing or any person in place of God means that all our relationships are askew. It can be argued that the whole of Judeo-Christian scripture can be understood as a warning against idolatry: "Put no gods before me" (Exodus 20:4, Matthew 4:10, Luke 4:8).

Our ability to compartmentalize our lives—into sacred and profane, or clean and unclean, or productive and unproductive, or "my tribe" and "not my tribe"—leads us down that idolatrous path. God's gift of creation, pronounced "good" at the very beginning, is the gift of wholeness, with everything existing in relationship with all creation's parts. What part of God are we willing to put on the profane/unclean/unproductive/"not my tribe" side of the ledger?

Peter's vision in Acts 10:9–16 ends with the warning from God, "What God has made clean, you must not call profane." Whether it's money or labor or sweat or trade or venture capital, labelling the by-product of honest toil can be dangerous.

When we decide that money is ungodly, we can all too easily quarantine our dealings with money into a realm outside God's domain. Putting our financial dealings outside God's line of sight demonstrates our foolish imagining that God would excuse, and perhaps overlook, the lack of love we might demonstrate when we interact with money.

Unfortunately, the long-term outcomes are never good when any god—and particularly Mammon, the god of money—is set in place of the God whose name is love. We lose sight of that inter-connectedness of God's creation and forget that money does not exist for our self-centered comfort or delight. Money, like everything else in God's world, exists to make the world a place of greater wholeness, and to delight God in the process.

Claiming Our Sacred Identity

In nearly all cultures, wealth bestows power: the power to buy, surely, and the power to delight ourselves in the process. It also brings the power to control, to exercise our will over others. That power to cause others to do our bidding can convince us that we are gods, shaping our environment to suit our needs and, often, overlooking the needs of others in the process. Sometimes the power of money can even exempt us from paying the price of what we do with our wealth, reinforcing our delusion. The power of money to fund our self-deception is limited only by the bottom line on our personal balance sheet. The temptation to equate that with our human value can be unrelenting.

Fresh from his baptism, Jesus offers us an example of resisting such temptation before he begins his active ministry. The three gospel stories of Jesus's temptation in the wilderness (Matthew 4:1–11, Mark 1:11–13, and Luke 4:1–14) show us Jesus confronting "the great deceiver" and demonstrating how resisting idolatry grounds us in right relationship with God. Richard Rohr offers his insights:

> I see the three temptations as the primal and universal temptations that all humans must face before they dare take on any kind of power—as Jesus is about to do. They are all temptations to the misuse of power for purposes

less than God's purpose. They are sequentially the misuse of practical everyday power, the misuse of religious power, and the misuse of political power.

But let me point out something we almost always fail to notice. We can only be tempted to something that is good on some level, partially good, or good for some, or just good for us and not for others.

Temptations are always about "good" things, or we could not be tempted: in these cases "bread," "Scripture," and "kingdoms in their magnificence." Most people's daily ethical choices are not between total good and total evil, but between various shades of good, a partial good that is wrongly perceived as an absolute good (because of the self as the central reference point), or even evil that disguises itself as good. These are what get us into trouble.[57]

The temptation to avoid claiming our role as stewards of all that we have and all that we are may be good for us and not for others. We can be tempted to turn over responsibility for our financial well-being to others and to God. Living as a spendthrift, without a thought for our future, may feel good, as long as someone else pays the bills and provides for whatever life might bring us. But a greater good—for us and for those around us—is claiming our own agency. "Adulting," as millennials term it.

We are tempted to undervalue our matchless worth in God's eyes and overvalue the things we put in God's place. We can choose to worship our wealth, or we can decide instead to worship God through our wealth. Instead of allowing money to become an idol, we can use it as a tool to accomplish God's work.

The former can deprive us of the things we most cherish; the latter can enable us to invest ourselves as we participate in the Beloved Community.

Money is an expression of value. As such, it can become an expression of who we are, and how we understand our identity. As Christians, we believe our identity is rooted in God.

Allowing God to help shape our relationship with money can offer a sense of freedom and life-giving power to believers. God's presence in our money lives brings a sense of freedom and agency in our management of our assets, and nurtures our growth in faith. Connection with a faith community offers both support and the opportunity to multiply the impact of our assets. When money can help us begin to see ourselves as beloved children of God, each of us created in love and endowed with sacred worth, then money can be holy.

4 ▪ *Why Does My Faith Community Care?*

"Everyone wants to ride with you in the limo, but what you want is someone who will take the bus with you when the limo breaks down."
—Oprah Winfrey

Claiming who we are, and whose we are, is a major task of our growth as Christians into "the full stature of Christ" (Ephesians 4:13). That growth is not solely an "inside job." Our participation in a community of believers shapes our lived understanding of God at work, especially through our relationships—with people, with human institutions, with God, and with our own spirits.

When we choose to become part of a faith community, we become part of a body, an expression of the Body of Christ. In that body, each member brings their relationships with family and friends, with their work, with the wider community, and, yes, even with money. Beyond those individual relationships, the faith community demonstrates through its mission and ministry how it chooses to engage with its members, its neighbors, and its money. Those relationships, both for the people and for the institution, are expressions of their identity.

Financial Discipleship

Steve Tomlinson coaches Wall Street, Fortune 500, and high-tech start-up executives and managers. He is also an associate professor of leadership and administration at the Episcopal Seminary of the Southwest and a founding master teacher at the Acton School of Business for Entrepreneurship.[58] He asks how all the energy and excitement that surround making money, participating in business, and all the things that are part of our stewardship of our gifts in the world, how all that is related to the expression of stewardship of our spiritual resources. He sees money management as a significant area where churches are called to shape their members in what he calls "financial discipleship." Tomlinson poses a provocative question in his webinar on the subject:

> Jesus warns that Money is God's most powerful competitor for our affection, devotion, and attention, that "Mammon" becomes god for us. So, if Money were your god, how would you know? Mammon's kingdom is based on scarcity, competition, unlimited desire, and the "usefulness" of others. In faith, we believe the world just works this way. The Gospel offers us compelling countercultural possibilities, but we find it hard to believe in the Kingdom of God.
>
> What if we tested these alternative possibilities in our behavior with money—spending, saving, getting, giving? What small experiments (risks and sacrifices that disrupt our habits with money) are we willing to try? How might such small experiments deepen our faith? Seeing how money can function as your god (how it can organize your thoughts, perception, fear, and aspiration; limit your responsiveness; direct your attention, and so on) can help you move towards the more loving and liberating God revealed in Christ.[59]

In the webinar, Tomlinson identifies some of Jesus's highly counter-cultural money experiments:

- Sell your possessions and give to the poor.
- Give to Caesar what belongs to Caesar.
- Give to everyone who asks of you.
- Carry no bag, no purse, no stick or sandals.
- Untie the donkey. The Master needs it.
- Give secretly.

He invites the participants to choose one of those challenges. In relation to that challenge, he asks them to chart their present behaviors and the beliefs that they reflect, and contrast them with future possible behaviors and their consequences. Tomlinson asks, "What would I need to believe in order to actually live this way?" And then he advocates finding a behavior that has a cost and a risk level that each experimenter can tolerate, in order to practice the behavior Jesus asks for. The experiments his students tried included:

- Tracking their expenditures, raising their awareness of how and why they spend money.
- Buying nothing for an entire day, raising awareness of what they do with that time.
- Paying attention to the hands and the eyes of those with whom they exchange money.
- Looking into the eyes of people who asked them for money, and allowing God to tell them what to do.

Practice in intentionally exposing ourselves to slight risks and refraining from customary almost-unconscious behaviors is most fruitful when undertaken in community. Peer support and group reflection—learning in community—can lead to long-term change in behavior. Tomlinson describes those intentional shifts in practice as a way of breaking the grip of the God of Money in our lives. Such small experiments can teach us that the "truths" of finance that we absorb from our culture—thinking about money as the thing that keeps us safe, or believing that our usefulness to other people determines our worth—are steps along the way to learning financial discipleship.

> Because Mammon is our culture's god—and often our own—practice with money is uniquely powerful formation for Christian discipleship. Instead of avoiding Jesus's tough teachings and ignoring impossible commandments, we can see them as opportunities for small experiments. We can apply whatever faith we might have to creative tests of his promises. With prayer and playful curiosity, we may discover that Kingdom thinking works in the real world, that money's illusions are optional, and that we can afford the luxury of a greater God.[60]

Churches can be prone to look on "discipleship" as a way of securing new members, and then look to new members to sustain a growing budget. Instead, Tomlinson asks faith communities to understand their work of "discipleship" as forming people who adopt a "following Jesus" lifestyle, being born into new lives that are shaped around practices that embody Jesus in every aspect of life. The practice of perceiving what we have in abundance and discerning how to use it as a life-giving resource is a discipline of that new life.

Practicing Stewardship

All too often, churches come to think of "stewardship" as referring to the season of fundraising many congregations observe each fall. Stewardship is not a season; it is a theology, an understanding of our relationship to money and to all that God has given. The practice is not synonymous with persuading congregation members to tithe—to make a gift of 10 percent of their income—in order to support the mission and ministry of their church. Instead, it is a posture of engaging with the world as a steward—a caretaker, nurturer, and guardian—of our resources.

Unlike the church world, the academic world and many other areas of fund development understand the term "stewardship" as focused on the donor. In those cultures, "stewarding the donor" means making sure the donor's wishes are honored and expressing gratitude to the donor in multiple ways, recognizing that their generosity makes possible the work of the institution. Ironically, such an understanding seems far more "Christian" than the way many churches talk about stewardship, particularly in the way it gives primary attention to the continuing relationship with the person who has made the gift. Timothy Siburg writes for the Center for Stewardship Leaders:

> . . . I believe that leadership is stewardship, and that stewardship leadership starts with thoughtful, routine planning and open discussions with all those involved. Then, leaders must model that consistent, guided stewardship.
>
> Too often churches jump to talking about giving to the church and miss talking about the decisions families make (and need to make) around the kitchen table before

considering how and what they will give to the church. For me, this means sharing how my stewardship starts at the kitchen table each month as we take stock of what we have to work with and how—together—we can steward that which God has entrusted to our care. Then, and only then, are we prepared to have broader conversations with our church community.[61]

Greg Meyer, lead pastor of Fabric, an ELCA congregation in the Twin Cities, advocates that churches should be in the business of teaching personal finance, which he understands as a spiritual practice.

Yes . . . there is a spiritual practice designed specifically for money. It's called a budget, and we churches are the perfect context to teach it. Here's why:

- We can address all the dimensions of money, possessions, and debt.
- We are also all fellow strugglers with money.
- We [churches] don't go away when the [personal finance] workshop ends.

No other institution/community can bring such a whole-life perspective to our complex relationship with wealth.[62]

Meyer reminds us that money is a deeply spiritual issue, that everyone struggles with their relationship with money, and that churches routinely ask for money, seeking increases in giving from people who are often living above their means. He makes the case that being good stewards of the people in the pews practically demands that churches engage in teaching about money, from a whole-life perspective. He asserts that money is a challenge for people of faith: "Money, wealth, and the possessions they provide represent a spiritual crisis separating people from their real values and desire to follow God; and the people in our churches are well aware it is a problem for them."[63] He credits his congregation's frank engagement with money as one of the reasons it is financially self-sustaining.

> We believed from the beginning that our job was to help people understand their finances from the deepest, fullest perspective, not convince them to give us money. We help people move from drowning (as money and debt make all the decisions in their lives), to getting their heads above water (where money begins to serve them), to soaring (so that every dollar and decision can be an expression of the hopes and values they hold and reflect in their entire lives—including at church).[64]

Teaching about money, especially its spiritual dimension, is a powerful tool for forming mature people of faith. The growth they experience is liberating and life-giving, particularly as they gain agency in their own lives. And Meyer's criteria offer a liberating definition of success with money—when people understand money as serving them, and understand money decisions as expressing their hopes and their values. That vision can be realized among those of us with limited assets, and doesn't depend on possessing unlimited wealth.

The Road to Freedom

We all know that lack of resources limits options. Escaping the tyranny of money offers freedom—particularly in the choices available, and especially in the ability to make intentional choices around how you want to participate in God's reign in and through your own life. Developing the knowledge, self-assurance, and discipline to take charge of your financial life, in whatever income bracket you find yourself, offers true freedom. Operating in the context of faith, many find it especially liberating to use their resources to make their community a better place for all who live there—to contribute to the common good.

In his book *Living in the Village*, author Ryan Mack celebrates a church in New Jersey that has been intentional in its teaching about money:

> On the fourth Sunday of each month, the congregation celebrates a concept called *Dfree*—no deficits, no debt, and no delinquencies. The goal is to internalize good financial management by members of the church. Three levels of classes provide budgeting, debt recovery, five-year debt-elimination plans, estate planning, and financial accountability. As members reach levels of success, there is celebration as part of the worship. The dual benefits of using godly principles regarding finances are that the people *and* the church experience overflow blessings. . . . Strong spiritual bases coupled with effective financial planning along with making a difference in growing a community are the fundamental results of faith, finance, and follow-through.[65]

Mack's point throughout the book is, in order to be free to participate fully in building up the community, individuals must first develop stability, including in their financial lives. Just as the airlines' advice to "put your own oxygen mask on first" reminds us, that stability equips people to offer their own unique gifts freely in ways that contribute to the long-term well-being of their community. The individual and the community are symbiotic partners in building and strengthening their own lives.

That partnership creates a mutual accountability that is a hallmark of the beloved community. As Walter Brueggemann reminds us in *Money and Possessions*, "When possessions or money are viewed as mine without accountability, then they may be deployed in destructive ways at the expense of the common good."[66] Participation in the beloved community carries with it an expectation that each of us will choose to act for the greater good of all.

Money is one of the ways that we exercise and demonstrate power. The ways we put our money to work for us proclaim—more articulately than any credal statement—what we believe and what values we live by. Community organizers often say, "Show me your checkbook and your calendar, and I can tell you your values."

Faith communities demonstrate their values in much the same way. Their budget proclaims their mission and vision in practical terms. When their published mission statement and their budget don't align, their credibility suffers. And beyond that, the congregation is apt to lose its sense of purpose and vitality. Congregations, just like the larger communities in which they reside, have a vested interest in shaping their members' relationships with money to be holy and life-giving.

Money as Expressive Medium

Just as money is a tool, money is an expression of value. Just as an artist uses paint to make visible a vision of the world, "money artists" use currency to "give flesh to" a vision. Philanthropists, entrepreneurs, and even venture capitalists—along with everyday folks—can choose to use money in ways that bring life to people and communities. The Good News is that we can choose to dethrone the God of Money from our hearts. That choice for right relationship can free us to worship instead a god of healing, resurrection, and beloved community. Communities of faith are uniquely positioned to support people in making that choice. And whenever that choice is made, communities are richer for it.

Archegos Capital Management, a venture capital fund, supports the Grace & Mercy Foundation, co-founded by Archegos founder Bill Hwang. The foundation operates from the same office as Archegos and makes grants as investments in the community. In New York City, it hosts Public Reading of Scripture and Just Show Up Christian book study events on a weekly basis.

Intrigued by the Grace & Mercy Foundation and its relationship to Archegos, Stephanie Loo, a 2018 graduate of The Wharton School at the University of Pennsylvania, took a position with the foundation. Christian Union, a Christian leadership development ministry, profiled Loo in a recent article:

> "Immediately, I was drawn to the impact that Archegos Capital Management and The Grace & Mercy Foundation have had through their thoughtful investments, both in the marketplace and in the philanthropic world," she said.

"Stephanie is very comfortable with both staff and partners from our for-profit and social profit sides of the firm," [Richelle] Bryan [Loo's direct manager] said. "She is well versed in many areas and is comfortable initiating conversations with people from all professional and cultural backgrounds. This is very important since we are integrated with the staff and work of Archegos in many different ways."

Loo is pleased to work for an organization where she can use her business background to help make investment decisions within the non-profit space. She also appreciates "the culture of excellence and integrity that runs throughout Archegos Capital Management and The Grace & Mercy Foundation."

"I have learned so much, both from the people I work with and from the practice of regularly being in Scripture and learning from great books," she said. "It is through this culture that we are able to see great investment results and returns, both in the for-profit and philanthropic world."[67]

Andy Mills serves as executive chairman and co-CEO of Archegos. Working through the Theology of Work Project, Mills has created Faith in Financial Services (FiFS) "to act as a catalyst for leaders of the financial services industry in New York City to change the very nature of our industry by making Christ more relevant in our workplaces and communities."[68] The FiFS community held a kick-off community building event in September 2019. Mills describes the vision for the group:

The vision for Faith in Financial Services is to have Christians in the financial services community impact positively their work place. We live in a world that's very tough to deal with and the work is very hard. As Christians we have something very significant to add. We tend to be cowed, and we tend not to be very forward looking in our thinking. The ideas of Faith in Financial Services is to provide that support and that community to allow us to become those people of faith.[69]

Money is a medium of expression, like paint or stone or music, that brings to life both value and vision. The ways we use our money become an expression of the way we see the world, what we understand the world to be, and what we believe it needs.

Our vision of ourselves and our community shapes the ways we choose to interact with the people and institutions we encounter. Faith communities support us in learning to make the world a richer place by choosing to use money and love people, rather than the reverse. When money is understood as a tool to build community, to serve the common good, then money can be holy.

5 ▪ How Can Money Be Liberating and Life-Giving?

> "When someone steals another's clothes, we call them a thief. Should we not give the same name to one who could clothe the naked and does not? The bread in your cupboard belongs to the hungry; the coat unused in your closet belongs to the one who needs it; the shoes rotting in your closet belong to the one who has no shoes; the money which you hoard up belongs to the poor."
>
> —Basil the Great

> "In ordinary life, we hardly realize that we receive a great deal more than we give, and that it is only with gratitude that life becomes rich."
>
> —Dietrich Bonhoeffer

It's pretty easy to see how sharing food or clothes or shoes with someone who doesn't have them can be, literally, life-giving. That kind of giving rewards both the giver and the receiver, in ways that are usually immediate and heart-warming. Supplying the "goods" of life is straightforward, and is the most basic level of "charity." That word has morphed into a pejorative in many people's minds, even though the source of the word (the Latin noun *caritas*) speaks of love for all—the kind of love demonstrated by saints and philanthropists. It's *caritas* that is named by the apostle Paul in 1 Corinthians 13:13: "And now faith, hope, and love abide, these three; and the greatest of these is love." Just as money can represent sweat or work or power, at its best, it can be love in solid form. Whether it buys a warm coat or school tuition or full payment of rent or utility bills, money can be life-giving, especially for those who live on the margins of financial stability. In those cases, money can be deployed as liberating power.

Dr. Martin Luther King Jr. said, "Power without love is reckless and abusive, and love without power is sentimental and anemic. Power at its best is love implementing the demands of justice, and justice at its best is power correcting everything that stands against love." Dr. Arthuree Wright, commenting on those words, explains,

> Dr. King's *beloved community* exhibits agape love, which, as the love of God operating in the human heart, seeks to "preserve and create community." Christ's mature followers love each other as well as those who persecute or do evil against them. Christians confront hate with love because agape love derives its essence from the cross of Christ, which brings redemptive power. This love does not accept injustice or evil as acceptable. Rather, it loves by way of justice, which ensures equity in access, participation, and flourishing for everyone.[70]

Wright's description of the Beloved Community is congruent with Jesus's concept of *shalom*, a Hebrew word sometimes translated as "peace" but more expansively understood as universal flourishing, wholeness, and delight. When we have a *shalem* heart (the adjective form of *shalom*), we demonstrate "an undivided attitude of wholeheartedness" (e.g., 2 Kings 20:3) and practice an inclusive love that extends to bad people as well as to good ones.[71]

Money can serve as a powerful tool for demonstrating agape love. Love with such aspirations is larger than random acts of kindness, or impulse donations to a charitable cause. It grows out of maturity, self-awareness, and deep compassion, and understands that because justice is the public face of love, manifesting such love requires deep engagement with supportive community and long-horizon commitments to working as an advocate for justice.

The Soul of Money

Lynne Twist founded the Soul of Money Institute, inspired by experiences in Africa and South America with The Hunger Project and the Pachamama Alliance. A recent newsletter offers this story, embellished with quotes from her book *The Soul of Money*:

> "In our interactions with the Achuar people of Ecuador and the other indigenous peoples with whom we now have begun to work, the message is the same: 'Change the dream.'" —*The Soul of Money*, p. 180
>
> Dreams are central to the way the Achuar perceive the world. They take their dreams very seriously.
>
> The Achuar believe we really can't change our everyday behaviors because they are rooted always in our dream for the future, and our actions will always be consistent with that dream.
>
> "Historically, the world as we have envisioned has seemed to be a world where fixed, finite resources are declining so fast that we must compete in any way and at any cost to be among the people who can survive and be on top." — *The Soul of Money*, p. 181

Most of us are living a dream in which all growth is good, regardless of the human and environmental costs. Now, as the Amazon burns, we must change our dream.

We need to see the world completely differently—as indigenous people do: a world that is totally sufficient, animated with spirit, intelligent, mystical, responsive, and creative.

Indigenous people like the Achuar see human beings as part of that great mystery, each of us having an infinite capacity to create, collaborate, and contribute. Indigenous people ask us to look at what our dream is doing to us and the world we live in: the plants, the animals, the sky, the water, each other.

"[The Achuar] may be inviting us, imploring us, to re-see that what we need is already and always there. As Gandhi said, 'There is enough for our need but not for our greed.'" —*The Soul of Money*, p. 182

What kind of dream are you living? And, if appropriate, how would you like to change your dream?[72]

Deepak Chopra describes Twist's impact: "Lynne Twist provides a unique, intelligent, and soul-centered look at how we can release the burden of having or not having money. She brings inspiration and possibility to an area of life that most of us believe is unchangeable."[73]

Inspiring that transformational shift toward hope is the focus of the institute's goals:

The Soul of Money Institute addresses the dysfunction and suffering that most people have in their relationship with money, and we are bringing a new level of consciousness to the way money impacts our life and society. The Soul of Money Institute was founded to create a context of sufficiency, responsibility, and integrity for individuals and organizations in their relationship with money.[74]

The institute's work is based on seven principles:

- Prosperity flows from sufficiency—the recognition of enough.
- Each individual makes a difference.
- What we appreciate appreciates.
- Collaboration generates prosperity.
- Our legacy is what we live—not what we leave.
- Gratefulness is the heart of generosity.
- Global citizenship is the natural outcome of an awakening consciousness.

The recognition of "enough" is a key principle that lays the foundation for the institute's insistence on collaboration across difference and its recognition of worth residing in the individual. Lynne Twist offers her principle of sufficiency:

When you let go of trying to get more of what you don't really need, which is what we're all trying to get more of, it frees up immense energy to make a difference with what you have.

This new set of assumptions or new context can create a whole new culture around money and around life. It can teach us how to be known for what we allocate rather than what we accumulate. It can teach us to be measured and measure others by our inner riches rather than our accumulation of outer riches. We can learn how to end charity as we know it and begin truly investing or being vested in a new future that will serve us all. Although we think there are people with money and people without it, the real truth is, money is a part of everyone's life from the poorest peasant to the wealthiest industrialist, the way we direct the money that comes through our lives defines us.

The American billionaire and the Guatemalan peasant farmer, the European industrialist and the Ethiopian grassroots leader can stand together in co-equal partnership and invest their time, energy, and financial resources in a new future for all of us, in a future that will serve us all.[75]

These insights around the power and the allure of possessions are not new. Ohiyesa (1858–1939), a Santee Sioux physician and writer, learned as a child that possessions can be debilitating. He was raised traditionally and then educated at Dartmouth College and Boston College medical school. As an adult he took the name Charles Alexander Eastman and, because of his First Nations lifeways and his experience of historic events, brought a unique, unfiltered voice to the stories and histories he wrote. Eastman remembers,

> It was our belief that the love of possessions is a weakness
> to be overcome. . . . Children must early learn the beauty
> of generosity. They are taught to give what they prize
> most, that they may taste the happiness of giving. . . .
> The Indians in their simplicity literally give away all that
> they have—to relatives, to guests of other tribes or clans,
> but above all to the poor and the aged, from whom they
> can hope for no return.[76]

Right relationships with our money, our possessions, our assets
open the door to our being able to use our resources in liberating
and life-giving ways. Recognizing that we are beloved of God
allows us to claim our identity as co-creators and stewards of all
that we have and all that we are. The temptation to reject that
identity, to avoid claiming our role as stewards, can imprison us
in focusing on ourselves. As free people, we can participate in the
Beloved Community, using the resources that we control for "the
healing of the nations" (Revelation 22:2).

Using Money Soulfully

Recovering from the messages of a money-focused culture—those
crazy-making cultural assumptions about money explored in chapter one—can begin with being willing to become more intentional
about our interactions with our assets. There are four major shifts
in consciousness that can help:

- **Make Gospel values your plumb line.** Jesus tells us
  to invite as dinner guests those who can't repay us.
  As Franciscan Richard Rohr reminds us, instead of a
  "meritocracy," punishment/reward economy, Jesus
  calls us to a gift economy, where "there is no

equivalence between what we give and how much we get. . . . Basically, to understand the gospel in its purity and in its transformative power, *we have to stop counting, measuring, and weighing.* We have to stop saying 'I deserve' and deciding who does not deserve. None of us 'deserve'! Can we do that? It's pretty hard . . . unless we've experienced infinite mercy and realize that *it's all a gift.*"[77]

- **Take agency.** Understanding ourselves as the ones who are in charge of the money in our own lives is key to shaping the life we want to live. That may not mean balancing a checkbook monthly, a time-honored practice that focused on making sure the arithmetic is correct. With online banking the norm for many people, the awareness fostered by checkbook-balancing more likely means being familiar with our account's transactions and checking them regularly. It may mean determining how to increase our income, if ends aren't meeting. It might mean setting goals for saving, or discovering how to reduce our expenses. All of these require decisions and follow-through, guided by those gospel values. We can recognize we are exercising agency when our money decisions consistently reflect our values and our hopes.

- **Seek advice.** Breaking the barrier of reluctance to talk about money frees us to become more comfortable and more proficient with money. And quite likely to realize that our issues with managing our assets are shared by many. Just growing in confidence about the ways we interact with money can help each of us be more realistic in our expectations and our strategies.

- **Practice being a giver.** Breaking the grip of *things* on our lives and on our imaginations is hard work. One way we can gain more freedom is adopting a regular, intentional practice of giving something away—perhaps, as Ohiyesa advised above, something we hold dear. Money might be one of those things. My experience of giving to my church each year, and each year increasing the amount, has done much to grow my faith. And it has certainly given me the opportunity to "taste the happiness of giving." At the same time, as I've become better at giving, I've found that the things I go without are not much missed.

As we work to make these shifts our consistent practice, we need to remember what we're trying to achieve. The goal in our interactions with money is not, perhaps counter-intuitively, to simply accumulate a lot of it and become rich. The goal, as in all of life, is to become the person God has created us to be, using all our resources as God intends—so that we may joyfully play our part in participating in the reign of God, the Beloved Community. The King Center calls the Beloved Community "a global vision in which all people can share in the wealth of the earth. In the Beloved Community, poverty, hunger, and homelessness will not be tolerated because international standards of human decency will not allow it."[78] A hallmark of the Beloved Community is seeking the common good, recognizing that, as King wrote, "Injustice anywhere is a threat to justice everywhere. We are caught in an inescapable network of mutuality, tied in a single garment of destiny. Whatever affects one directly, affects all indirectly."[79]

Roman Catholic author Arthur Hippler defines the common good as "a good that can be shared in by all and does not diminish when it is divided."[80] As the *Encyclopedia Britannica* explains, ". . . the common good is a denial that society is and should be composed of atomized individuals living in isolation from one another. Instead, its proponents have asserted that people can and should live their lives as citizens deeply embedded in social relationships."[81]

"The common good" is a concept rooted in early Christianity. Fourth-century archbishop and noted preacher John Chrysostom wrote, "This is the rule of most perfect Christianity, its most exact definition, its highest point, namely, the seeking of the common good . . . for nothing can so make a person an imitator of Christ as caring for his neighbors."[82]

Andy Crouch, editor of *Christianity Today*, adds, "Seeking the common good in its deepest sense means continually insisting that persons are of infinite worth—worth more than any system, any institution, or any cause. Societies are graded on a curve, with the fate of the most vulnerable given the most weight, because the fate of the most vulnerable tells us whether a society truly values persons as ends or just as means to an end."[83]

Creating a relationship with money that is both healthy and holy means being mindful of the common good—of creating *shalom*, Beloved Community—as we exercise the power of the money that we control. That calls for us to hear Lynne Twist's Soul of

Money vision, the one inspired by her interactions with the Achuar, indigenous peoples of the Amazon Basin: "I have seen that we must redream, learn to question the cultural dream of 'more' and begin to create a dream that is consistent with our reverence for life."[84] As we create that new dream, Twist also calls on us to remember, "Having 'enough' is not an amount, it's a state of being."[85]

Getting to that state of being, that "land of enough," is a lifelong journey for many of us. Taking charge of our money life is an essential skill to develop. So is learning to experience and express gratitude as an everyday practice, and finding companions who will walk with us on the way. Cultivating a willingness to travel light makes any journey easier. When we're tempted to imagine that changing our relationship with money is like moving a mountain, John Paul Lederach's haiku offers sage advice:

> Don't ask the mountain
> to move. Just take a pebble
> each time you visit.[86]

Recognizing that money can be holy—that it can be used in holy ways to achieve holy ends—will not multiply the amount in our bank account. But it will help us begin to realize that we are wealthy. We begin to access that wealth whenever we choose to live our lives in ways that both demonstrate our love for people and deploy money as a tool of transformation.

Notes

1 Eli Cook, "How Money Became the Measure of Everything," *The Atlantic* (October 19, 2017), https://www.theatlantic.com/business/archive/2017/10/money-measure-everything-pricing-progress/543345/.

2 Ibid.

3 Ibid.

4 Keith Hart, "Money from a Cultural Point of View," *HAU: Journal of Ethnographic Theory* 5, no. 2 (Autumn 2015): 411–16, doi:10.14318/hau5.2.026.

5 Mary Cross, *The Emotional Life of Money: How Money Changes the Way We Think and Feel* (Santa Barbara, CA: Praeger, 2017), 92–93 (Nook edition).

6 Michael S. Malone, "Money and the Meaning of Life," *Fast Company* (June 30, 1997), accessed December 31, 2018, https://www.fastcompany.com/28699/money-and-meaning-life.

7 Eric Mack, "The Exact Amount of Money It Takes to Make a Person Happy Just Got an Update," *Inc.com* (February 16, 2018), accessed September 5, 2019, https://www.inc.com/eric-mack/the-exact-amount-of-money-it-takes-to-make-a-person-happy-just-got-an-update.html.

8 Ibid.

9 P.M. Ruberton, J. Gladstone, and S. Lyubomirsky, "How Your Bank Balance Buys Happiness: The Importance of 'Cash on Hand' to Life Satisfaction," *Emotion* 16 no. 5 (2016): 575–80, doi:10.1037/emo0000184, accessed September 19, 2019, https://psycnet.apa.org/record/2016-17475-001.

10 Daniel B. Kline, "How Much Money Do You Need to be Happy?" *The Motley Fool* (April 12, 2019), accessed September 19, 2019, https://www.fool.com/investing/2019/04/15/how-much-money-do-you-need-to-be-happy.aspx.

11 Ibid.

12 Dan Hotchkiss, *Ministry and Money* (Herndon, VA: The Alban Institute, 2002), 8.

13 Oxfam, "Richest 1 Percent Captured 82 Percent of Wealth Created Last Year While Poorest Half of the World Got Nothing," *OxfamAmerica.org*, accessed December 31, 2018, https://www.oxfamamerica.org/

explore/stories/richest-1-percent-cap-
tured-82-percent-of-wealth-created-
last-year-while-poorest-half-of-the-
world-got-nothing-1/.

14 John Nolte, "Trickle Down:
Starbucks Workers Win Pay
Raises, Expanded Benefits Thanks
to Trump Tax Plan," *Breitbart.
com*, accessed December 31, 2018,
http://www.breitbart.com/
big-government/2018/01/24/
trickle-starbucks-workers-win-pay-
raises-expanded-benefits-thanks-
trump-tax-plan/.

15 Lil Scrappy, *Addicted to Money*,
DTP Records, 2009.

16 "Ain't About the Money," an
episode of the *Empire* television series,
season 2.

17 Carl Richards, "How to
Talk About Money," *The New
York Times*, accessed September
23, 2019, https://www.nytimes.
com/guides/year-of-living-better/
how-to-talk-about-money.

18 Tammy Lally, "Money Shame:
The Silent Killer," TEDxOrlando,
August 22, 2017, 4:05, accessed
September 23, 2019, https://www.
youtube.com/watch?v=RxBfPDq8V
F4&feature=youtu.be.

19 Kristin Wong, "We're All Afraid
to Talk About Money. Here's How

to Break the Taboo," *The New York
Times* (August 28, 2018), https://
www.nytimes.com/2018/08/28/
smarter-living/how-to-talk-about-
money.html.

20 Ibid.

21 Bradley T. Klontz and Sonya L.
Britt, "How Clients' Money Scripts
Influence Their Financial Behaviors,"
Financial Planning Association,
accessed September 28, 2019, https://
www.onefpa.org/journal/Pages/
How%20Clients%E2%80%99%20
Money%20Scripts%20Predict%20
Their%20Financial%20Behaviors.aspx.

22 Tim Herrera, "What to Do
When You're Bad with Money,"
The New York Times (August 27,
2018), https://www.nytimes.
com/2018/08/27/smarter-living/
how-to-be-better-at-money.html.

23 Ibid.

24 Wong, "We're All Afraid …."

25 Maria Teresa Hart, "Navigat-
ing the Financial Side of a Relationship," *The New York Times*
(November 30, 2017), accessed
October 6, 2019, https://www.
nytimes.com/2017/11/30/smarter-
living/dating-financial-advice.
html?module=inline.

26 Ibid.

27 David Weliver, "How to Have 'The Talk': Six Tips for Couples Discussing Finances," Money Under 30 (April 19, 2019), accessed October 5, 2019, https://www.moneyunder30.com/money-talks.

28 Cross, *The Emotional Life of Money*, 89.

29 Weliver, "How to Have 'The Talk.'"

30 Geoff Williams and Coryanne Hicks, "How to Choose a Financial Advisor," *U.S. News* (March 11, 2019), accessed October 5, 2019, https://money.usnews.com/investing/investing-101/articles/how-to-choose-a-financial-advisor.

31 Ibid.

32 Zack Friedman, "9 Simple Money Rules All on 1 Index Card," *Forbes* (March 9, 2017), https://www.forbes.com/sites/zackfriedman/2017/03/09/9-money-rules-index-card/#4e843c862c09.

33 Stephen J. Dubner, "Everything You Always Wanted to Know About Money (But Were Afraid to Ask)," episode 298 of *Freakonomics,* August 2, 2017, http://freakonomics.com/podcast/everything-always-wanted-know-money-afraid-ask/.

34 Ibid.

35 Hart, "Money from a Cultural Point of View."

36 Greg Meyer, "Should Churches Teach Personal Finance (Part 1)," *The Faith+Leader*, Luther Seminary, accessed August 20, 2019, https://faithlead.luthersem.edu/should-churches-teach-personal-finance-part-1/.

37 Brené Brown, *Daring Greatly: How the Courage to Be Vulnerable Transforms the Way We Live, Love, Parent, and Lead* (New York: Avery, 2012).

38 Maggie Germano, "How to Cope with Your Money Shame," The Ladders personal finance site (February 21, 2019), https://www.theladders.com/career-advice/how-to-cope-with-money-shame.

39 Brené Brown, "Courage Over Comfort: Rumbling with Shame, Accountability, and Failure at Work," https://brenebrown.com/articles/2018/03/13/courage-comfort-rumbling-shame-accountability-failure-work/.

40 Kelsey Piper, "Bill Gates Is Committed to Giving Away His Fortune—But He Keeps Getting Richer," *Vox* (April 23, 2019), accessed September 11, 2019, https://www.vox.com/future-

perfect/2018/12/11/18129580/
gates-donations-charity-billionaire-
philanthropy.

41 "History of the Pledge," The
Giving Pledge, accessed September
11, 2019, https://givingpledge.org/
About.aspx.

42 Ibid.

43 Ibid.

44 Ibid.

45 Kelsey Piper, "The Giving
Pledge, the Campaign to Change
Billionaire Philanthropy,
Explained," *Vox* (July 10, 2019),
https://www.vox.com/future-
perfect/2019/7/10/18693578/
gates-buffett-giving-pledge-billion-
aire-philanthropy.

46 Marc Gunther, "Has the
Giving Pledge Changed Philanthropy?," *The Chronicle of
Philanthropy* (June 4, 2019),
https://www.philanthropy.com/
interactives/20190604-givingpledge.

47 Ibid.

48 Jesse Wisniewski, "Bible Verses
About Money: 9 Practical Principles
You Need to Know," *Tithe.ly*, accessed
October 12, 2019, https://get.tithe.
ly/blog/bible-verses-about-money.

49 Claude Mariottini, "Walter Brueggemann on Money and

Possessions," https://claudemariottini.
com/2016/11/15/walter-bruegge-
mann-on-money-and-possessions/.

50 Fleur Dorrell, "How the Bible
Helps Us Work for the Common
Good," *Christianity Today* (April 26,
2017), https://www.christiantoday.
com/article/how-the-bible-helps-us-
work-for-the-common-good/107947.
htm.

51 Stephen W. Hiemstra, "Brueggemann's Bible Follows the Money,"
t2pneuma.net (July 10, 2018), 9–10,
https://t2pneuma.net/2018/07/10/
brueggemanns-bible-follows-the-
money/.

52 Ibid.

53 Ibid.

54 Felix G. Rohatyn, "Ethics in
America's Money Culture, *The New
York Times* (June 2, 1987), https://
www.nytimes.com/1987/06/03/
opinion/ethics-in-america-s-money-
culture.html.

55 The King Center, "The King
Philosophy," accessed October 20,
2019, https://thekingcenter.org/
king-philosophy/.

56 The Episcopal Church,
"Becoming Beloved Community:
The Episcopal Church's Long-Term
Commitment to Racial Healing,

Reconciliation, and Justice," accessed October 13, 2019, https://episcopalchurch.org/files/becoming_beloved_community_vision_english_0.pdf, page 5.

57 Richard Rohr, "Lent with Richard Rohr: Temptations Are Attractions to Partial Goods," Franciscan Media (March 10, 2019), https://blog.franciscanmedia.org/franciscanspirit/lent-with-richard-rohr-temptations-are-attractions-to-partial-goods.

58 Steven Tomlinson, "About," accessed November 2, 2019, http://steventomlinson.com/about/.

59 Steven Tomlinson, "Testing Mammon: Learning Financial Discipleship," webinar, April 25, 2018, https://www.ecfvp.org/webinars/231/testing-mammon-learning-financial-discipleship.

60 Steven Tomlinson, "Testing Mammon: Learning Financial Discipleship," ECF Vital Practices, May 2017, https://www.ecfvp.org/vestrypapers/article/619/testing-mammon-learning-financial-discipleship.

61 Timothy Siburg, "Pancakes," in *Stewardship 101: An Invitation to Financial Stewardship,* Center for Stewardship Leaders, Luther Seminary, accessed August 20, 2019, https://ss-usa.s3.amazonaws.

com/c/308466932/media/67185ced54945150e504409580/Stewardship101_online_2018.pdf, page 33.

62 Meyer, "Should Churches Teach Personal Finance (Part 1)."

63 Greg Meyer, "Should Churches Teach Personal Finance (Part 2), *The Faith+Leader*, Luther Seminary, accessed August 27, 2019, https://faithlead.luthersem.edu/should-churches-teach-personal-finance-part-2/.

64 Ibid.

65 Ryan C. Mack, *Living in the Village: Build Your Financial Future and Strengthen Your Community* (New York: St. Martin's Griffin, 2010), 40 (Nook edition).

66 Walter Brueggemann, *Money and Possessions: Interpretation: Resources for the Use of Scripture in the Church* (Louisville: Westminster John Knox Press, 2016), 5.

67 Tom Campisi, "Extending Grace and Mercy," *Christian Union*, Winter 2019, https://www.christianunion.org/publications-media/christian-union-the-magazine/current-issue/2189-extending-grace-and-mercy.

68 Theology of Work Project, "What Is Faith in Financial Services?,"

accessed November 18, 2019, https://www.theologyofwork.org/resources/what-is-faith-in-financial-services.

69 Theology of Work Project, "Andy Mills' Vision for Faith in Financial Services," transcribed from video, accessed November 18, 2019, https://www.theologyofwork.org/resources/andy-mills-vision-for-faith-in-financial-services.

70 Arthuree Wright, "25 Traits of the Beloved Community," Religion and Race—the United Methodist Church, accessed November 1, 2019, http://www.gcorr.org/25-traits-of-the-beloved-community/.

71 Leslie Allen, "Shalom as Wholeness: Embracing the Broad Biblical Message," *FULLER Studio*, accessed November 25, 2019, https://fullerstudio.fuller.edu/shalom-as-wholeness-embracing-the-broad-biblical-message/.

72 Lynne Twist, Wednesday Wisdom, October 23, 2019, newsletter of the Soul of Money, https://www.facebook.com/sharer/sharer.php?u=https%3A%2F%2Fmailchimp%2Fsoulofmoney%2Fchange-the-dream.

73 Soul of Money, "About the Soul of Money Institute," accessed November 19, 2019, https://soulofmoney.org/about-2/soul-of-money/.

74 Ibid.

75 Lynne Twist, "Sufficiency Is Not Abundance," *Awakin.org*, accessed November 13, 2019, http://www.awakin.org/read/view.php?tid=2097.

76 "Charles Alexander Eastman," Goodreads, accessed November 23, 2019, https://www.goodreads.com/author/show/135759.Charles_Alexander_Eastman.

77 Richard Rohr, Daily Meditation, November 24, 2019, Center for Action and Contemplation, https://www.facebook.com/pg/CenterforActionandContemplation/posts/.

78 The King Center, "The Beloved Community," accessed November 25, 2019, https://thekingcenter.org/king-philosophy/.

79 The Rev. Martin Luther King Jr., "Letter from a Birmingham Jail," African Studies Center, University of Pennsylvania, accessed November 25, 2019, https://www.africa.upenn.edu/Articles_Gen/Letter_Birmingham.html.

80 John M. DeJak, "Seeking the Common Good," *Distributist Review* (November 26, 2011), accessed November 23, 2019, https://distributistreview.com/seeking-the-common-good/.

81 Simon Lee, "Common Good," *The Encyclopedia Britannica*, accessed November 23, 2019.

82 Jim Wallis, "Whatever Happened to the 'Common Good'?" *Time* (April 4, 2013), http://ideas.time.com/2013/04/04/whatever-happened-to-the-common-good/.

83 Andy Crouch, "What's So Great About 'the Common Good'?" *Christianity Today* (October 12, 2012), https://www.christianitytoday.com/ct/2012/november/whats-so-great-about-common-good.html.

84 Twist, Wednesday Wisdom, October 23, 2019.

85 Lynne Twist, "The Soul of Money," *goop* podcast, accessed November 18, 2019, https://podcasts.apple.com/au/podcast/the-soul-of-money/id1352546554?i=1000440125104.

86 John Paul Lederach, "Poetry from the On Being Gathering," *On Being with Krista Tippett*, October 1, 2018 (transcript), https://onbeing.org/programs/poetry-from-the-on-being-gathering-john-paul-lederach-oct2018/.